A Soul Untameable

Fine Words Weave

Azeezat Adeola A B A

ISBN: **9798410116251**

I believe that all the words that will ever be
written in love
are gift wrapped messages from The Most
High,
so I start this project with
Bismillah
May any good in it be accepted of me.

Dear reader,

These are love letters
from my soul to yours.

With love.

Author's Note

Dear Beautiful Soul,

Thank you for deciding to purchase this collection of poems, I sincerely hope they are of benefit to you. I am prefacing this book with an invitation coupled with some ideas about how the poems can be used as reflective tools, if you so choose. As well as letting you know how to contact me or share anything that comes up for you from this work, and where you can hear me speak Black Girl's Flight Plan for free, before the audio book is out.

I'm a big believer in the power of self reflection, and the ways that writing can be a useful tool for that. Many of the poems in this book do speak to strong and deep feelings, and questions around power, placement in society, questions about self connection, and the necessity of being heard and appreciated. I am mindful that this content could bring a lot up for readers, and am a big advocate of talking to people trained in supporting people in mental wellbeing and embodiment. Please talk to someone trained in this work, if you feel the need for support.

Now for the suggestion on ways to use the poems as starting points for reflection.

Reading the poems out loud: This can be really useful in experiencing the power your voice can have.

Changing the pronouns in the poems: sometimes parts of the poems will speak in the second person voice, it can be powerful reading the poems and seeing how it feels changing it into a first person poem, I know from experience (shout out to my therapist) that the way the poems sit with me changes when I do this.

Journalling: It could be really useful to see what comes up for you after reading any of the poems, and just writing down your thoughts and reflections on those thoughts can be a great tool to get a deeper sense of your impressions, and could reveal things about yourself you had not consciously considered.

Painting, drawing: if you are artistically inclined, (and even if you're not!) you might feel moved to express your impressions of the poems in other artistic mediums. Even as someone who's visual artistry skills has its limitations, I know how therapeutic art can be, so I really like the idea of inviting you to try this.

If you choose too engage in any of these invitations and would like to share any of what you create with me you can email info@finewordsweave.com, or you can use the

#ASoulUntameable for related shares on social media.

The audio version of this book is imminent! I think there's something really important (for me) and powerful in putting my voice to the words, when I wrote the poems, I hear them in my head first and during that process. If you would like to hear Black Girl's Flight Plan in it's audio format for free, you can listen to it on the very first episode of my podcast Fine Words Weave. You can find this podcast on and of your favourite podcast hosting platforms.

Happy Reading,
With Warmth

Azeezat

PART ONE

UPTURNING WATERLOGGED SOIL

How To Undelicate A Flower

The story starts
Much in the way
That many stories do.
    It starts with hope,
So full and buoyant
that it fills the flower up.
Its petals rapidly unfurling
To drink the sunlight
Of this hope.
    This hope is
Sun beams
And sweet nothings.
A look here,
A connection there.
And the flower,
Thirsty,
Hungry,
Attention starved—

Believes
That all its summers
Have come at once.
  That the dry,
Cold, hard,
Frost of desolate winters,
Lack of connection,
Misunderstanding and despair,
Has finally passed.
  And this—
This warm and
This light
And this heat
Will be
Its time
To grow and glow
  It's the idea
Of the thing
The idea of hope
That keeps
The flower
Open
  Even as
The weather
Turns mercurial
And the sky
Turns obsidian
And the temperature plummets
  The flower
Clings on
To the idea of hope
  As dark days
Cloud in
Again and again

The flowers petals
Turn brittle
  And then a day
Of weak sunlight
Of hope
  And then
More dark
Bleak sunless days
  And then
a brilliant summer
A surprise of heat
And warmth
  It is this sporadic
Uncertain
Unsafe
That undelicates
The flower
  The flower grows
Thorny
And wary
And soon wise,
But that poem
Is not today
  Today
The flower still thinks
That you
Are the sun
That your light
Is the only source
Of growth.
  The flower yet
Has Learning
And Growing
To do.

A Soul Untameable

Vulnerable Tendencies

The underside of the petal,
Is not softer or silkier
But something inside me says it's more delicate
More prone to tearing.

And when you my lovely
When you are that underneath
And they try to rip away
Your self belief

It all so readily comes undone
You might not even notice the rip
So busy are you
Trying to keep yourself
From being waterlogged
So busy are you
Seeking some form of nourishment from the sun

That your awareness
Dances past the fact
That the underside of your petals
Are dangerously close
To tearing free

Your face and petals
Are turned towards the light
So focused on photosynthesis
You don't notice the approaching night

Picked Apart

Every word that fell
    From my lips
    Had the unenvied
    Task of standing before you

To be eyed
    And measured
    Just picked apart
    And held up
    Against the standard
    Of how you believed i ought
    To talk.

Never mind
    That the words i selected,
    Had already
    Been through several filters
    Before they reached the gate
    Of my mouth
    Tumbled over the hill of my tongue
    And fell from my lips

Never mind that these words
   Tumbled straight from my heart

What ive learnt
   Is the danger
   In letting my words be
   Ratified
   By someone
   Without the capacity
   To truly hear how my heart speaks

Wound

Peel back the layers
   Of an unhealed wound

Expose the gory
   Guts of things
   For the viewing pleasure of the world

They feed on it
   And you are left
   Empty and hollow
   Raw and wounded

Sometimes you need
   To let it breathe
   Let the blood touch air
   Congeal and scab over
   Give yourself time and room to heal

Wrapped in a bandage
   Soaked in salt water
   Whatever it takes

Then you can speak

Of this old battle wound
　　Of how the war almost killed you
　　But here you are
　　To live and tell the tale

Speaking of what lessons you learnt
　　On your wild adventure
　　How you know what it is to live
　　Having so very nearly tasted death

How you count your blessings everyday
　　That your skin is coming in now
　　The scab flaking off

The scar might fade,
　　but never the experience
　　And the lessons you learnt

So wait,
　　At the first breaking of skin
　　Wait before you expose it,
　　To keep it from festering
　　Sometimes you must let it breathe

A Choice

It serves you
For me
To be a delicate flower
Petals unfurling
Beautiful to behold
And easy to crush
    Releasing my scent
In each fisted hand
Perfuming you
Even as you
Make pulp of me.
-
It doesn't serve me
What you will find
Are steel veined petals
And thorns and barbs.
    Blood in your hand
As your fist curls
For the crush
    I release my scent
When and how I will.

I am not here
Yours for the
Taking
My beauty
is not yours
It belongs
To The Divine.
And what
It serves me
to notice
Is that
This choice
Is mine

Space To Grow

It's time I let you Go
    So I can have the space to grow
    Your roots have choked me so
    I've been in your stronghold
    And now I'm breaking free
    Won't let you keep hold of me

Anymore

I am enriched by the earth
    I have buried all the things we shared
    And as our relationship
    Decomposes
    Deep in the soil
    I strip the nutrients
    The learnings are blessings

I take these lessons
    And I am fertilised and nourished
    A new growth
    Stronger than I've ever been before

Yes there is salt water in this soil
   Yes my tears and blood
   But I open my mouth
   And I say no to you

No to your limits
   No to being a succulent host
   To your parasitic control

And yes to me
   Yes to growth
   Yes to the sunlight
   Shining down on me

Yes to feeding myself
   Yes to my hearts health
   Yes to choice
   And autonomy

Yes to breaking free

If A Girl Falls In The Forest

If a girl falls in the forest,
    But no man was around to hear it
    Did she make a sound

If your ears are blocked
    To the sounds of her screams
    Is she still screaming?

I am so sick and tired
    Of this convoluted narrative
    Where a man is worth his word
    Yet a woman's word has no weight
    Unless counter measured by a man

The words I tell you in confidence
    But you have no confidence in me
    In the things I tell you
    About my confinement
    In the morals and values
    Of this time and place

The weight of the world is on woman's shoulders
    And she takes and she takes
    Until she's ready to break
    And sometimes the breaking is her only deliverance

The splitting of a seed
    Premeditates it's growth
    The splitting of a woman
    Premeditates the birth
    Of a newness
    A tempered glow

Tested by man's fire
    Again and again
    Until she is willing to take no more

She bathes in that tempered glow
    Molten fire waters her soul

No More Footstools

Mmm mmm mmm
    Mmmm mmm mmm

A Black woman
    Was martyred today
    So today
    Is a day like any other
    The days my eyes have seen
    same days like my mother's
    And hers before her

The expectation
    That I as a black woman
    Should be satisfied
    With the sound
    Crack
    As my back breaks
    From the burden of every person
    I have carried.

Constant talk
    Of
    standing on the shoulders of giants
    And no one looks to see
    Blackened brown
    Gleaming backs
    Folded and stacked
    As foot stools for those so called giants

Can you be called a giant,
    If a Black woman's back had to break before you raised
yourself high
    Bodies on the podium
    Built from our bodies
    It must be crack

I meant you really must be high
    These are the lies
    That are lullabied to black girls
    Who grow up to become Black women
    Who grow up to become foot soldiers
    And footstools
    In the endless climbing
    Towards
    Everyone's mutual destruction

Do you see us as fools?
    Because eye,
    My eyes, have seen things
    And my throat,
    is closed
    Scar tissue built up
    From all the screaming,
    The chanting

The yelling,
Til' my voice is left at a hum.

Mm mm mmm
   When does
   The Black women rest

Mmm mmm mmm
   When does she
   Rest

Mm mm mmm
   I bow my back
   And touch the feet

Of another Black woman martyred
   Mmm mmm mmm

And my prayer is to never see
   Another Black woman
   Be the foot stool for a giant

PART TWO

BURNING WINGS, CHURNING SEAS

Something Brown

Something brown
    Something black and blue
    Somehow picked apart
    And knocked about
    By life
    By man
    By the draw of the cards

But underneath something golden
    Something undefeated
    A girl
    A woman
    Full of heart

She wrapped herself
    Around her child
    To protect him from the dark

The dark tried to eat her
    But she is life

And she is spark

She doesn't see it yet
    But I know
    She holds the fire
    Of life inside her

She has enough heat
    To burn it all
    To smithereens if she chooses
    And open up new channels of light
    Sparkly bright new paths

The dark and cold of this life
    Has seeped into her brittle bones
    Her breath is condensation clouds
    Smoky in the air

And she feels the cold
    Something black and blue

I am her friend
    She is my sister
    I let my spark blaze
    To keep her warm

I want her to know
    She has a comrade in arms
    As she soldiers on
    Something brown

I watch her back as she rest
    Arms wrapped tight around her child

I too have lived parts of her story
    And it's truly heartbreaking
    That anyone should have to live it at all

But I know
    She is something golden
    And that she will ultimately find her spark
    And set the world alight

Out Of The Ashes

Out of the Ashes she emerges
    The embers still smouldering
    On her burnt down pride,
    Leaving her vulnerable
    Yet free from her hard shell life

She surveys her surroundings
    The landscape looks different now
    The haze of smoke
    A sooty shadow over the things
    That had been weighing her soul down.

A thin layer of dust
    And a cloudy coating
    But she sees clearer now
    Than ere before this time
    And gratitude shakes her frame

Has her tumbling down
    first to her knees
    Then lower still

Her head humbly kissing the floor
In sujood (prostration) to her Lord

She had felt so broken
    In the depths of despair,
    But this fire has razed
    The very things holding her back
    Stopping her from recognising khayr (goodness)

From recalling her mission
    Her primary goal
    That lies in her submission
    To the One in control of it all.
    He Controls it All.

She sucks in a smoky breath
    Her lungs are aching,
    From the tears that ravaged
    As much as the burning
    They cleansed too though

And she is so grateful
    For reaching this place
    This opportunity for learning
    low as she is
    It's the perfect opportunity to rise
    This time in Grace.

She is humbled and hopeful
    That what she builds now
    Will be in better standing
    Steeled by the furnace

Of unwavering tawakkul (trust)

That has her tranquilly tumbling down
    first to her knees
    Then lower still
    Her head humbly kissing the floor
    In sujood (prostration) to her Lord

The thin layer of dust
    Is a cloudy coating
    Which she sees clearer now
    Than ere before this time
    And gratitude shakes her frame

She surveys her surroundings
    The landscape looks different now
    The haze of smoke
    A sooty shadow over the things
    That had been weighing her soul down

Out of the Ashes she emerges
    The embers still smouldering
    On her burnt down pride,
    Leaving her vulnerable
    And free from her hard shell life

Missing Myself

I look in the mirror
    Dark brown eyes stare back
    They're a bit damp and
    My cheeks are puffy
    Yet my lips tilt up in to a smile
    Hey miss girl
    It's been a while
    Since I saw you

I mean it's been ages
    Since I really took the time
    To see you
    To acknowledge
    That person
    Staring me boldly in the eyes

So **on** with the hustle and grind
    That I just forget to take the time
    To switch off
    Unwind
    Climb down from the conveyor belt

And re-connect
I mean really connect with myself

I told you I was going to show up this year
Be more intentional
Really build you something special
And you took the promises in stride
Was it ignorant of me to think
That the special thing I needed
Was outside

There's a pain that comes
It pulls apart the expanse of my chest
Shallows my breath
The type of hollow breathing you do
When you've been neglecting yourself
I've been missing myself lately

And myself has been patiently waiting for me to come back

Black Girl's Flight Plan

I feel this first in the bottom of my throat
    It feels like a hollow
    Then A shallow tremble flutters from my solar plexus
    down to the clenching in my gut.

And I am tired
    although I've rested,
    Because I wonder if there's enough rest in this life
    That will keep a black woman uplifted and replenished.

Divest from the discourse.
    The gender war
    And all the controversy

My skin will not be fodder
    For the pyre they are burning.

You see being stripped of my skin
    Is not a new sensation.
    I remember sticks and stones may break my bones
    But words would pull strips from me.

The little darks skinned
    black Girl in the playground,
    Gleaming like a gem,
    That flash of white teeth,
    Set in a dark face
    Like the white stones
    We'd dig out of the concrete

Was a siren for magpies
    And so the magpies came
    To pick apart what they could,
    To steel anything that glimmered

Medusa they cawed,
    When they saw how I'd picked apart
    My irun shuku (a yoruba hair style).

Shuku meant
    The pulling of my scalp on a sunday evening,
    The tap of an ilarun (comb) on my head,
    As my mum reminded me
    Don't let anyone touch your hair.
    The eternal temptation to unplait my rows
    To undo my crown,
    So I too might fit the magpie's standards

That I might blend in.

I was never made to blend in.

Outstanding as a black girl
    sometimes means
    You just stand out.

Too talkative
    the hen teachers clucked
    Adeola must stop distracting others.
    The un crowed subtext being
    Smaller little black girl

How dare you show up in all your light
    Don't you know
    You can only glow
    When we add you to the pyre.
    When we can benefit from your warmth and wingspan

As I speak now
    My heart accelerates,
    Like the thundering after the bleep test,
    Or the one in your chest
    When you get on the bad side of your parent,
    And the sensation is one
    Of danger.
    Of fear,
    Saliva filling your mouth,
    In anticipation of pain.

Orokpo
    The nick name They gave me at home
    It means your talk is too much

It means
  your talk is too much

And when I'd talk back
    I'd get a lip twist in conditioning,
    In negative association,
    In if you don't hear you will feel
    in home training
    For the war out there
    But what that meant
    Is that I learnt to bite my tongue

I mean literally bite my tongue.
    Sinking my teeth in,
    till my tongue was warm
    And numb
    And my mouth filled with saliva.

So I mean it when I say
    I've tried and tested,
    Shrinking into myself,
    To become more palatable.
    And I wonder if there are enough people with vested
interest
    In a black woman being uplifted and replenished

And at this point my body knows the answer,
    Because people loved
    To use my body
    As fuel for that bonfire
    To lift them up,
    Elevated on the back of a black girl

And when I was in what I thought
    Was a loving relationship with a black man
    Because black love
    And you complete me
    And this is half your deen and
    I want to be seen

He opened his mouth,
    From within his beard
    And it turned into a beak
    As he squawked
    So you want to grow wings?

And this one felt like just too much
    The last straw on the black girls black

It felt like squaring up
    And when will I rest?
    And if I open my mouth
    The whole earth will tremble

And who said I
    Black girl
    Who said that I
    Have no right to wings
    To soaring
    And flying
    Swooping freely far beyond the reach of those
    That would have my body
    As a log in the fire

The gender war
    Sharp shooters
    Would rather

Blitz
Spitfire
Have me in their sights
And bring my body all the way back down to
set in stone earth.

And now it feels
Like my shoulders drawn forward
My body leaning into the wind
My big laps
I mean these thick thighs
Gearing up
For the run of my life
Unclench my jaw
On the runway
And lift off into flight
Because flight fight freeze fawn

I'm not a worm or a pawn
Not bird fodder
Nor funeral blacks
The smoking ashes
Open my mouth
And I refuse to call these words back

Let
the earth
shake.

Because I black woman
Am resting.

And I'm tired

Of holding it all up.

And if I have to leave this life behind
    The one of
    Strong black girl myths and legends,
    If that means that I will be uplifted and replenished.

You'd be blessed to see the tail end of me
    As I loop the loop in the sky.
    Turned into the morning's swallow

Yes I've grown wings,
    But let me tell you
    they've always been there
    And the hens and crows and magpies
    All the other birds
    Tried to clip them.

And now I black girl,
    uncontained swallow
    am fluttering towards
    This world's solar plexus.

And I am in your gut.
    And I know that you are hollow.
    And I burst out,
    Know
    that I've got all the smoke,

My glow
    my light
    my fire
    Is beyond fodder for your desire.

Breath Filled Bodies

You spoke over my spirit
In an attempt to capsize
Little did you know
That like all breath filled bodies
Eventually
I will rise

I am the rise
And the fall
And in each of those states
I still swim beyond
The seas of your vitriol

Your jealousy and petty
Churn only within you
No capacity to
Hold self to account
Yet a seasoned sailor

In blaming those around you
For all the misgivings
The tempests in your life

I can see why
At one time we were a fit
In the depths
Of mental illness
That mindset
Reflected
On your seemingly placid surfaces
Was familiar and welcome

Yet as I sank deeper
Seeing the ocean floor
The decision grabbed hold of me
I can sink into this no more
So I propelled myself to the surface
Lungs burning
On the way up

Front crawled my way back to breathing
The current let me up
Freely gliding on the surface
Island's safety in sight

Taught through experience
That some submit to it
The dragging of their lower self
A whirlpool
The sucking gurgling
Of an unaware self
Unbalanced
And in the worst health

And to tangle with one such,
   coupled with the blurred lines
   Of self delineation
   The tidal waves of empathy
   Without boundaries

Is to offer myself
   To the drowning,
   That they might catch hold of me
   Pulling me under too
   Not reaching for the surfaces
   For a return to breath
   No rather in their desperation
   Of air cutting off,
   In their drowning
   They would sink me too

And I would be the fool
   Without comprehension
   That I have to get to the life boat
   Or the island of safety
   In order to launch a rescue mission
   And actually some drowning
   Don't actually want to be rescued

Some drowning would like to see my lips turn blue
   Does melanated skin
   Turn blue?
   The thought bubbles up
   The way the most inane ones do
   Occurring to you
   as the blackout comes

Then awareness shakes me
    And I remember this is life and death
    That if I let it take hold of me
    If I sink into the depths
    It's a long swim up
    And the more times I sink
    The longer the journey to the surface seems to take

I've got people waiting for me
    On safety island
    Small people who depend on me
    The will to live
    Burns deep in my belly
    Fuelling my need to navigate
    Towards home built on land

I've seen the bottom of the ocean
    I know what lurks deep within
    And I've let go before
    And mercifully my body has risen to the surface
    Floating because it's full of breath

But the fear of the ocean floor
    Is not to be taken lightly
    I have faith that I will always rise
    That knowledge doesn't do anything to the unpleasantry
that is sinking
    The squeeze as your lungs burn
    Oxygen depleting
    The horror of inhaling water

So I've learnt many a lessons
    On the seven seas

And lesson number one
Is to never offer myself to the drowning

I let the waves pulse in my ears
    Drowning out your words
    Bubbled out in desperation
    They depict a person you once knew
    Not the woman I've front crawled my way to becoming

A woman who knows
    How far down the ocean floor is
    A woman who's touched its sand
    Made a home and rested in seabed
    A titan who's swam back up to the surface so many times
    I'm almost a mermaid
    Though I've not traded legs of the land
    For sea ones yet

It's something I refuse to do
    I will never sacrifice my voice for a drowning man
    Who would see me drown
    Before taking account
    Turnings arms to oars
    And swimming himself back to
    Breath

Your jealousy and petty
    Churn only within you
    No capacity to
    Hold self to account
    Yet a seasoned sailor
    In blaming those around you
    For all the misgivings
    The tempests in your life

I am the rise
  And the fall
  And in each of those states
  I still swim beyond
  The seas of your vitriol

Sea legs
  And land legs
  A seasoned
  Deep sea diver

You spoke over my spirit
  In an attempt to capsize
  Little did you know
  That like all breath filled bodies
  Eventually
  I will rise

Standing, Still

I am standing still
    And I dont want to talk
    I am in need of steadiness
    And silence

As I stand and witness
    This constellation of oppression
    And injustice
    And suppression
    Of everything that is human

The sparks and charge
    Of conflict
    Multiple flickering flames
    In the darkness
    Of what this world has become

Anger washes over me in waves
    And waves
    And waves
    And waves

It is slow,
    And thrumming,
    And pulsing,
    And i must be still
    In order to hold on to
    Some semblance of safety

Because safety is something
    Tricky and slippery
    Not a fur wrapped around the neck
    But us clawing onto its
    Oil slicked surface

With my head raised skywards
    The sense is that safety is a birth right
    But in the body of my experience
    It's something that has been denied me and mine

And the trauma lives inside of me
    Of eyes wide open
    Watching the darkness
    Squeeze the breath
    From human spirit after human spirit

Of death chasing us
    And us running simultaneously
    away from and towards it.

I want to shut my eyes
    To all the things I've seen
    The things I'm yet to see
    Of brutality and blatant wrongdoing
    I need to shut my eyes to it

For now they are pried open
    In guilt and solidarity
    The weight of survival,
    Carrying the memory
    Of those that didn't
    Dragging the love for them
    That filled your heart behind you
    It's a carcass on your back
    How dare you try to turn your back on witnessing what
must be witnessed

So your eyes remain open
    Can't help but see the pattern
    In this dark smattering of sparks
    On a blanket of sky
    As they pic nic,
    Idyllically
    As safety starved bodies
    Swing from trees

And the strain of that slick rope
    Cutting through the air echoes it sounds
    Across the night

Standing still
    Yet still moving forward
    I can do nothing but witness this
    Again and again

I can do nothing
    But stand as witness
    I am standing still
    In witnessing the sinking of capitalistic vanity

And the rise and rebirth
Of our interconnected humanity

And the fatigue that comes with this
Recognising the spirit of subjugation
In different iterations. And the knowing
That there's more of this to uncover
You've seen the galaxy,
Interlinking threads
That tie it all together

We are all tied together
And the tide
Washes over me
In waves and waves
And waves and waves

I stand, still
Wanting a quietness,
A grounding
A way to be centred
As the earthquake
Shakes the foundation
Of crumbling decayed institutions

A strong conviction that
The dawn will break the sky
That the end must be nigh
That the light
Will be blinding
And wash away sight

Unseeing

You'll come back to witness
the constellation of oppression,
and it will have changed its shape

You hope

That charges and sparks
    The burning flames will
    Flicker instead with life
    And love
    And the right to safety inside our bodies

Now though, you are tired
    And you take solace in
    this exhaustion.
    It is Personal progress,
    Allowing yourself to rest
    It speaks to your starry night journey

It says I live inside my body now
    I no longer flee the pain
    I trust my self to withstand
    Though it's still a work in progress

I know there are others
    Who grasp my hand
    And we collectively
    Stand
    In witnessing
    What must be witnessed

We take it in shifts
    Holding silence
    With a recognition

Of what lies in the heart of being
The potential For great love
We wrap love as cloaks around ourselves
To offset the chill of the darkness

I am standing still
And will continue too
Even when it all burns away
Even when I feel the collective pain
None of us escape accountability in the end

I am standing still
And I dont want to talk
I am in need of steadiness
And silence

An Unstormable Knowing

One more round with the tempest.
   She stands,
   arms outstretched in a daring embrace,
   as she locks gaze with the eye of the storm.

 Energy jitters up her spine,
   and her tongue is dry.
   She's danced this whirl wind before.

Spun out over and over,
   leaving breathless and dizzy,
   that's if she even leaves at all.

The tempest calls her name,
   blowing temptingly in her ears.
   Drawing her in just a bit.

One foot forward,
   without conscious thought,
   she's already in forward motion.

Pulled in by the deceptive calm.

Still the weathered shawl of foreboding
    settles on her shoulders,
    and her skin pinpricks
    with that quiet un-nameable sense,
    that something is just out of step here.

She's been around this tempest before,
    this isn't her first spin,
    and lately she's tired of letting herself
    be reeled back in.

Emotionally battered,
    mind windswept,
    she's intimately familiar
    with the post-storm landscape.

The tempest howls,
    the wind buffets at her mind,
    the noise is reaching crescendo.

She turns inwards
    to the quiet within.
    And asks a single question.

The answer makes steel rods of her legs
    and she is at a stand still.

The question?

Is this.
    what you want ?
    for your life?

Lightning fizzles from within the tempest,
    aiming at her stock still legs.
    There is pain and tingling,
    and the metal taste of hot electricity.
    As the bolt hits at where she is grounded.

Is this what you want for your life?

Honestly,
    the answer is so quiet,
    It's hard to hear it beneath the roar of the storm.

 Still it matters not,
    because the answer becomes her vision.
    She feels it right in the gaps.
    She unstormably knows the answer
    in every fiber of her.

She is steady as the tempest rolls over.
    It flails and roars,
    wails and hails.
    Steadily drags at her core.

It comes with dark
    and thunder
    and shuddering.
    Shaky teeth,
    and the shivering.

The storm is a mighty thing.
    The knowing within is mightier still,
    and she does not let the storm in.

She draws deep from within herself,
  The strength to weather it.
  At moments her legs falter,
  and at times she is almost carried away
  by the force of the storm,
  still the unstormable knowing
  is her steadying.

The storm does its worst.
  The knowing is unstormable.
  The tempest passes.
  She stands still.

Her arms outstretched in an open embrace.
  The storm has subsided.
  And faintly she hears a new question.
  What do you want for your life?

Shadows In The Light

Step by step
    Im walkin a sombrely pebbled path
    To sit
    with the shadows in the light

My journey is to be present
    To the darkness that stretches a smile

You see the careful warmth and glow
    Can be the shop front
    To a storeroom filled with gloom

People polish their sparkle
    Looking away from their dim

You know we have to learn to acknowledge
    The wild flickering

Beneath the open trapped sky
    The fog beyond the warmth
    The white chalk outline

I will sit with you whilst you explore
The space inside the closed doors

Washed Anew

Tap in to something true
    And abundant

Give over
    Yourself

Heart and soul
    To that which is Divine

Notice the sensation
    A coursing vibration

It thrums through
    Washing you anew

This is life
    Coming to recognition
    Of the divine

Heart and soul
    Give yourself over

In abundance
 Tap in to truth

Nurturing Love

I am learning to nurture love
   From a seed to a blossoming thing

Blooming and shedding,
   Season by season
   Until one day it's not just a bud nor a shoot
   But a massive tree
   spreading it's branches
   Giving us shade
   Relief in the heat and hardships of life

But I am not a gardner
   I have the opposite of a green thumb
   I've mostly seen how to nurture weeds,
   Like greed and hurt
   Nurturing the wounded feeling

Still I am determined to learn
   How to nurture love
   Not just in others

But firstly in myself

From a seed to a blossoming thing
    Blooming inside me
    Leaves turning over
    Season by season
    Til one day its a massive tree
    With branches spreading out
    Sharing it's shade

This life has lots of water
    I know my heart is fertile ground
    For this love to grow
    If i'm brave enough to nurture it
    Let go of the hurt
    Pluck it out before the weed gets stronger
    And nurture
    nurture this love.

Because the truth is
    It's not anything I do
    That will nurture the love,
    It's just opening my heart
    And planting the seed
    Accepting the water when it comes
    Intending the best

And I think
    That's how I will learn
    To nurture love
    From a seed to a blossoming thing
    Blooming in my hea

Discovering Poetry

Discovery of poetry
    I hear the words beneath my skin
    The words I've had to swallow
    The truth that simmers within

The discovery of poetry
    Is finding the valve
    An outlet
    Of what simmers within my spirit

The steam of all that lives pouring out.
    And in this elimination
    I discover myself anew
    Uncovering
    Lessons
    And meanings
    To all the things we live through

So an ode to the poets
    Who go from life
    To death

And back to living
Signs that
It's written that we
Will all be revived

An ode the poets
Who do the witnessing
Words spilling out
What many would
Wish to shove in to the un-see

The poet says
All that occurs
Must come before the light
Uncovered even if
Those that push things down
Might wish it otherwise

In the mouth of a poet
Truth runs free
It is spectacular
And welcome
People click fingers
And chime in
With mmhmm
Spit your truth
Kinfolk

PART THREE

SOARING AS WATERS POUR FROM THE SKY

Let The Bluebells Bloom

My mind reminds me

To be more careful now
With my heart

She is open
And always yearning
For connection
And shared understanding

But heart and mind have learnt
That there must be
Boundaries

Gated brick walls
That open
When the criteria
Of a discerning soul
Has been met

The alone lonely
Of childhood
Has heart craving,
Seeking

Wherever she finds understanding
She extends herself
attachment

So mind reminds her
To take her time
To be mindful
There is time

See how things unfold
Let the bluebells slowly bloom
To be in reception
Is different from lack

How I Feed My Soul

I feed my soul
    By drinking at the water
    Of my gifts

I feed my soul by
    connecting with the flow of it

It's renewed from the source
    Of life

And every time
    I tap into intuition

Every time I stand at the waterfall
    Of the deep water
    That connects us all

I feed my soul
    By being in
    Connection
    With the life

That flows through us all

Present

You'll never know
    What the room was like
    Before you entered it

You'll never know
    What the world was like before you burst into it

And you'll never know
    What the world will be like, after your dip

You'll never know
    What the room will be like
    After you've left it

You do know,
    What it is,
    Right now
    At this moment.

You don't live in the future
    Nor do you live in the past

You are here in the present
    Baby
    Your presence is
    A divine gift
    To all who receive it

Words, Voiced

The words
    Will be there
    When you need them

Exactly When you need them
    Not a moment before

Trust
    That
    The power
    That gave
    Animation to your form

Will give sound
    And body
    To your voice

The words will be there
    At exactly the moment
    You need them

Remembering How To Float

You dip your head beneath the water
    And automatically your chest constricts
    The pressure around your throat
    Has you bobbing out again
    In discomfort

We are born knowing how to swim
    From all the floating in amniotic fluid
    As we learn to crawl
    Then walk on land
    To struggle and survive
    The capacity to let go
    To float
    Is lost to many of us

So we take swimming lessons
    To teach us anew
    Something that instinctively we once knew

There's a knack to breathing
    Whilst beset by so much water

It clicks when you get
into the rhythm of it
Stroke after stroke
Your head turning just so

Inhale
Dip your head
Stroke stroke
Exhale
Air bubbles
from the mouth
Stroke stroke
Nose seeking oxygen
Fill your chest
Stroke stroke
Inhale
Stroke stoke
Exhale
Stroke stroke

You see
It begins to come
naturally with practice

It is no longer resistance
It's letting go
Learning to float
When all things have capsized
And you are beset by water

Inhale stroke stroke
Exhale stroke stoke
Let go
Stroke stroke

Float

Release

When your soul comes home
    To the vessel that is your body
    Create space for integration
    In welcome
    Heart and soul
    greet each-other

Balloons filled with
    All the things
    That no longer serve you
    Hands hold the strings
    Open palms
    Release
    Eyes trailing them
    As they float up into the sky
    You thank them for being here
    The wisdom they imparted
    Your heart open
    As you witness their departure

You are witnessing

And you are witnessed

Ups and Frowns

These ups and frowns
    This too and fro
    Riding the coaster
    Caught in emotional throes
    The one thing I've learnt
    In this dual poled journey
    Is the only way out is through

To feel the feelings
    And let them breathe
    Even if that means
    Sitting still laughing and crying
    In a state others might term manic

The thing is
    I've learnt my specific brand of crazy
    I know it's a week out of the month
    Where I dance
    Like a puppet on a string
    To the tune of
    Raging waves of feeling

I know not to make decisions
    And to talk myself down
    To not expect productivity
    And to block this time out

To feel all the things
    To fully submerge myself
    In the tidal wave

Not fighting the tide
    Just making space
    For this feeling
    Unfeeling
    Until i swim my
    way back to equilibrium

Embodiment

I love it when
    I'm physically in my body
    When I feel how my feet's roots extend into the earth
    Every-time they hit the ground
    The pulling of my calf muscle
    When I flex my foot arch

When I can consciously feel the curve of my shoulder blades
    and the sweep of my neck
    When I inhale and feel it in my lower stomach and back

The sensation of my eyelids moving
    When I blink

My body is an orchestra of sensory input and output
    Being embodied is a gift
    The musical score
    Of being in tune with yourself

Kiss The Sky

Stand in the rain,
   dance as the water hits your skin
   Things have been hard of late

Buttoned up
   In the norms of society
   Laugh as the rain kisses your face

You are wild
   You are blessed
   The heaven opens
   Sending down nourishment

Gratefully receive
   Knowing that each drop
   That lands on your body
   Is carved with your name

All the water
   And riches that drench you
   Have your moniker

Inscribed on them

They meet you
    Where you stand
    The conclusion
    Of a story
    Written before now

I know things have been hard of late
    So dance as the water hits your skin
    Stand in the rain
    And kiss the sky

Kiss The Earth That Birthed You

Kiss the earth that birthed you
    Sink to your knees
    Toes entrenched in the earth
    Digging deep
    Knees touching soil
    Lips a gentle press
    To the place of growth

Your tears salt water
    Lands
    And the roots drink deep from your well

Do you know that you are constructed from the same
material
    That all that is lush and green grows in

You were born from earth
    And it's to terra you will return
    Before you go

Make sure you've planted your seed

Made your mark
Contributed to green
And growing

As you press your lips to the ground
Remember you have a duty
To leave something behind
Of the lessons you've found

Be a part of the life cycle
That your life in its ending
Can be fertiliser
For growth
Still yet pending

So kiss the earth
You were birthed from
This land is your birth right

Standards

These are my
    Self defined standards
    Of how I will be treated
    I need not justify them

And it is within my rights
    To see them enforced
    In a way that causes no harm
    Whilst also securing my right to safety

My acknowledgement of my autonomy
    And how I desire to be treated
    My very own how to be in my company charter
    The legislation of my human rights

What I will and will not tolerate
    What I've ratified as mandate

You need not comply

Know though,
    There are consequences
    To resistance
    And non-compliance

My company is a privilege
    And I am within my rights to withdraw it

Should I feel you don't appreciate it
    I refuse to be tolerated
    I am deserving of so much more

Certainly

Sometimes the dusk can get so dark
    That I find myself sitting
    Unsure about the sunrise

I've sat in the dark
    Accompanied by grief and despair
    The melancholy whistle of hopelessness
    And lost vision

And the cold of every miss step
    Mistakes I've mistook

And whilst this is true
    Whilst the stars find their places
    Smattered across the great inky dark

I have sat still in the darkness long enough

To know that uncertainty about the sunrise
Doesn't stop the dawn from breaking

It doesn't stop the white thread of morning
Distinguishing itself from night
It doesn't stop the birds' hopeful chorus
As they sing in the day's dawning

And no matter how uncertain I am
About the golden light
crowing the dark
The sun will rise
Certainly

Made Of Earth (Tremble)

I know that seeds are cultivated
By farmers or maybe food growers
I vaguely remember geography class
Discussing GMO produce.
There are silos somewhere of seeds
Deemed important, should crops fail globally.
    And I know
That the seeds of my life
Are rooted in the experiences
Of those that came before me
And the experiences of my life
Are fodder for the seeds to come.
    I know that we are all connected
Made of earth
We all tremble
When life shakes us.
    I know that water nourishes us.
Both fresh water and salty tears
In the same ways that sun (light)
truth and respect are nurturing.

When I dig in the soil,
Of what has gone
And I edge cautiously
Around the hurt
The bewildered rage
And the deep desire
To have been protected
    I come back to myself,
And think about how
Many people
In the body of my family tree
Have been touched by similar experiences.
    I know that we are all connected
Made of earth
We all tremble
When life shakes us.
    I drew a genogram in class one day
Is there an equivalent of this for plants?
A record of people and relationships,
Of life and death, and who branches from where.
Stories of origin in pictorial form.
    And when I could see it all in front of me,
I noticed a pattern.
Of miscarriages and death.
Of people departed
Before they were delivered on earth.
    I had to dig to find this.
Remembering it for me,
There's something about echo
Experiences reverberating
Repeating until they are resolved.
    I know that we are all connected
Made of earth

We all tremble
When life shakes us.
   And they say that trembling is healing
Sometimes in response to trauma.
I think of it as the buzz
Of the nervous system resetting.
They say that humming is healing.
They both go hand in hand,
Releasing all that tension.
   I know that we are all connected
Made of earth
We all tremble
When life shakes us.

For The Trees Who Touch The Sky

For the tress who touch the sky
    Who stretch out
    Limbs yearning
    Towards the freedom
    Of the days painted canvas

I salute you
    Your agelessness
    You perseverance in growth
    As my eyes touch sight
    Of your branches spread proudly

I can not know
    The intricacies of your story

How many a thunder storm
    Struck you down?
    How many a tree doctor
    Performed open trunk surgery?

All I see
　Is your radiance and splendour
　Your magnificence. And courage
　For stretching always to wards the sky
　Your journey
　Providing shade for all
　Who sit beneath you

The lessons to be found
　In the story of the tree stretching towards the sky
　Are as numerous as all the leaves
　Sitting and fallling from branches
　On all the trees shrubs and plants
　On this lush green planet

But just for this moment
　Whilst my eyes behold you
　I breathe inspired
　Experience you as a
　Sign of hope

You are proof of potential
　How tiny green shoots
　Can split the earth
　And with time
　Nourishment
　Perseverance
　And patience
　Can touch the
　Multi-hued
　Cloud softened
　Ceiling of the world

Cleansing Love

I am standing on the coast
    It is ice along the horizon
    White blue pink gold
    My breath puffs with the cold

My breath comes in with the tide
    And I exhale as the tide recedes

Tears warm my cheeks
    As I embrace a cleansing love

I channel it
    Sending out that love
    The compassion
    The embracing acceptance
    Of all the pain and injustice

The rage and the uncomely
    I pour and pour the love
    And it floods back my way
    On the return

To the earth
    To the roots
    To the people

I know that love is not lost
    I know that all those that survived
    Are so wrapped and embraced in love

I know that even the particles in the air
    Vibrate with love and peace
    Calling us all back
    To restoration, truth, and harmony

My eyes trace the waters lapping the shore
    As the tide goes out once more
    And I exhale
    I notice all the tiny shells
    The sparkly things
    On the shore

The bed of the land
    Beneath the waters
    I know there are
    Innumerable treasures

My breath comes in with the tide
    And I exhale as the tide recedes

My breath puffs with the cold
    White blue pink gold
    It is ice along the horizon
    I am standing on the coast

A Soul Untameable

They say you grow from your experiences
    That the things you go through
    Have the ability to mould and shape you.

If you are buried in the soil of
    What you have been through.
    Then your soul is
    The spark of life within a seed

Faith is the sun,
    The casing splits asunder,
    and you
    push through
    the dark soil
    of experience,

Green and fresh

Splitting the earth,
Reaching towards the sky,
Soaring high,
Abundant new life
Grows from you

Truth always comes to light.
    Breaking darkness,
    Much in the same way
    Mama Dawn breaks
    the dark of night.

The fact of the mother is
    My soul was shaped before
    I reached this plain
    It was fashioned by the most High
    To make it capable of seeking Him
    Through and beyond its pain

This is a soul
    That man was unable to tame
    And it was placed in the body
    Of a woman.

This
    Woman

I'm planted before you
    Words growing out of my mouth
    The song of my life so far,
    A blooming heir to the legacy
    Of my mothers before me

That I suckled resilience

At the breast of life
That I suckled strength
And resistance
In the face of strife.
That these are the minerals
My roots absorb

That the trauma that tried to
Cut of my souls oxygen
was the same spark
that ignited
The furnace
Of faith
And knowledge
Intertwined to bloom
Into certainty

Of the strength I'm blessed with
Of the source of my power
Of the vibrant
And energy
And life
Zinging through every particle
That makes up my element

I said we are in our element
Everyday reclaiming our power
Ours are souls untameable
shaped by the most High
Singing the songs of our mothers

Every note
Falling like raindrops
A flooding of love

Nourishing our souls
As the sun of faith feeds us
We split the earth
Green
Anew
A forest of life

Pushing through
The soil of experience

Souls untameable
Will always find their way
Towards the light.

This poem is for me
And it's for you,
It's a song
That we received as lullabies
Your soul
Is untameable.

Acknowwledgements

Gratitude:

To the Divine, for gifting me with language, and expression. Words and poetry have ,and I imagine always will be, a much appreciated gift and means of coming to know my feelings, truths, and lessons.

I dreamed of being an author, ever since I was a little girl.

Thank you dear reader for reading the writings of my soul , and being a part of fulfilling my childhood dreams.

To my mum, who I inherited the bookworm gene from.

To family and friends who put books in my hands, listened to my voice, and encouraged me.

To the squishes, the eldest of whom said "mum, give yourself a pat on the back" upon seeing me complete my manuscript, and the youngest of whom gave me a squishy little hugs. I love you both abundantly, and I hope that seeing me achieve my dreams teaches you both that you are just as, if not more capable of doing so, and I hope to be a support you in those efforts, whatever your dreams may be.

To Felicia Cade,
who asked "who are you talking to"
and spoke her poems with such soul and power, that I was moved spiritually,
who told me 86 poems was not too much, and who was happy to do a read through of this poetry collection.

To all the poets I met on CH, where I rediscovered my poetic voice, thank you, for sharing space, and your words, for laughing into the late hours, for moving me to tears somedays, for teaching me, by example how to be more vulnerable in my poetry, and for reminding me to "leave empty".

To my OG poetry boo, love you sis, thank you for always pouring into me, and affirming my voice.
To The Black Women who are regulars in A Minute With Arah (CH) for soul nourishing conversations, warmth, and community.

To The Ripple Community & it's founder for a place to come and breathe five days a week.

To the Poetess Queens, who gave a private audience to my first poetry reading, at the end of an open mic, on top of a little black box of a seat, after the mic had been unplugged, who got it when I said "why have I just been sitting inside with my words and not taking them out and sharing".

To BYOB my first ever open mic- of the above mentioned, little black boxes, and to Poet's Corner, where I got to share my poems, on a stage for the very first time, and feel my poetry move through me, and to Rumi's Cave Open Mic, and the Poetic Collective.

To the "I'm Tired" gorlies
for being second eyes on my book cover.

To my sand/ soul/ earth/ clay sisters.
Who's souls recognised mine as soon as we met. There are only a few of you that I've met (so far), but you've made my life so much richer. The tacit understanding of a person who's often found herself misunderstood, has been a balm to my heart and soul in many ways. May your efforts, love and acceptance, be rewarded with abundant good, ameen.

And lastly to myself, for showing up, afraid, uncertain, unwilling, tentative, hopeful, dreamy, living through my darkest days, hopeful, joyously, laughingly. Thank you for learning to show up for yourself. I know you didn't imagine you'd make it through, but you did, and here are some of the poems that speak to that.

Printed in Great Britain
by Amazon